Deep wounds

Shamela Dad

Shamela Dad

ISBN: 1985728869
ISBN-13: 978-1985728868

DEDICATION

I know that I'm an adult and I may not act like it at times.
But it has never failed me to recognise how much you have done for me throughout the years.

Mum, thank you for making me realise that I'm worth everything in this world and much more.
You showed me that I must be treated like a queen, and that I should never settle for less than what I deserve.

Dad, thank you for telling me what I'm capable of. You gave me the support that I needed to build and achieve my dreams. You showed me that I have the talent to reach my goals.

Shamela Dad

CONTENTS

Deep wounds

Shamela Dad

ACKNOWLEDGMENTS

There are a few people I would like to thank.
Without them, this book would not have happened.
Firstly, I would like to thank my parents for their
unconditional love and support during this journey.
Secondly, a big thank you to the Instagram writers who
were involved in writing a piece for mental health
awareness:

@saifwrites
@thesmilingakh
@rollsroses
@hk.writes
@xsywritesx
@unpublishedwords
@sami.388
@akhthatwrites_
@Saidnotspoken

Book cover credit – Instagram- @mitch_gr

Shamela Dad

Pain

Shamela Dad

Once upon a time,

-    I opened my heart to you.

Deep wounds

It's ironic how the same love which saved me,

-     is now drowning me.

Shamela Dad

He was hell.
A beautiful hell,

-     that I didn't mind getting burned in.

Deep wounds

I thought you would be my happy ever after;
but now,

-    you are my once upon a time.

Shamela Dad

He was a demon,

\-   that fed off my love.

Deep wounds

There is no difference between my feelings and the ocean.
I am surrounded by the darkness of the deep, blue sea.
The tides pull me back in the same way my feelings do.
Sometimes it's easier,

- to drown in the ocean.

Shamela Dad

When I was with you all I felt was peace.
Now that you're gone,

-     I'm left in pieces.

Deep wounds

I cannot forget the day you walked out my life.
You left me bleeding,

-      with the shattered pieces of your promises.

Shamela Dad

I find myself drowning,

-    in the ocean of your words.

Deep wounds

Gasping for air yet I'm still breathing.
Drowning yet I'm still alive.
I want to escape your thoughts that pull me away from the light.
They take me to a darkness,

-    The deepest parts of my soul.

Shamela Dad

My heart is a graveyard buried with your thoughts.
They died on the battleground,

-    with lost dreams and hope.

Deep wounds

As the dark night closes in,
I feel your memories smothering and suffocating me.

-       drowning me once again.

Shamela Dad

I was drowning but then I met you.
I thought you were going to save me.
But instead you pulled me in deeper, watched me
suffocate.
I could no longer move.

-    I could no longer breathe.

Deep wounds

I would rather have all my bones snapped and broken than having to suffer the pain of a broken heart.

- It's crazy right?

Shamela Dad

Why do you have the need to lie?
You do the complete opposite.
You make promises yet break them.
You say you won't hurt me anymore,
yet you do.
Here I am,
a broken soul,

-    drowning in crushed hopes.

Deep wounds

I have overdosed.

-     on your thoughts

Shamela Dad

I feel blinded by fear.
I am drowning in doubt.
Looking to escape,

-    there is no way out.

Deep wounds

Slowly, slowly.
Piece by piece,
my love for you,

-      ruined me.

Shamela Dad

Every part of me is intensified to the point of excruciating
pain.
That pain is nothing compared to the uncontrollable
craving,

-    for your love.

Deep wounds

Your love is a powerful drug,

-     which I ache for compulsively.

Shamela Dad

It pains me ever so much when I hear the words
'forget them and move on.'
Don't they understand?
It's difficult to forget the one who turned my prickly
thorns into a red rose of passion.

- How do I forget the one who helped me bloom?

Deep wounds

They say-
 you don't know what you have got until it's gone.
What if I was fully aware of what I had?
What if I appreciated every single second?
What if I tried my very best to hold on?
Isn't it such a torturous hell knowing I had everything?
Yet now I could only look on helplessly.

  -   I lost the person who meant the world to me.

Shamela Dad

They say that within time the pain will disappear.
But no matter what I do, the pain haunts me inside.
I can feel it clutching on to my chest as it rips out my heart
in shreds.
So, tell me,
is it the pain we fear so badly
that we create an illusion in our heads
that forces us to believe that the pain will disappear?

-   But does it really?

Deep wounds

I'm mourning over love,

-    which was never there.

Shamela Dad

I'm sorry.
I'm sorry I am not the reason behind your smile.
I'm sorry I am not what you need.
I'm sorry I was selfish.
I'm sorry I made some bad choices.

-     But I will never apologise for loving you.

Deep wounds

You were my home,

-   Now I'm homeless.

Shamela Dad

Do you remember when you told me how much you love
the rain?
It rains every time I cry.
Maybe that's the reason you remain happy while I hurt.
In the hope of you enjoying the rain,

-    I will forever endure the tears and the pain.

Deep wounds

I will go through hell,

- to keep you happy.

Shamela Dad

One day my physical wounds will heal.
But here I am praying,

-    one day my shattered heart will mend too.

Deep wounds

I can feel the unstoppable
agonising pain.

-        deep within the core of my soul

Shamela Dad

Words spoken can lead to hearts being broken.

-    It is best to remain silent.

Deep wounds

I was infuriated by the treacherous quicksand of life.
I could not find a way to escape.
But then you came along with a rope.
I thought you would pull me out and save me.

-      You used the same rope to tie a noose.

Shamela Dad

I miss you ever so much that it pains me.
So easily you walked away.
Now I sit here at war with my dreams and reality.
Praying and begging that you return to me.
Can you not feel the love which we felt anymore?
Have you forgotten about our dreams?
Come back to me,

-   I would do anything.

Deep wounds

Loving you went from a blessing,

-    to a curse.

Shamela Dad

I would give you a piece of me every single time.
And now,
 I'm left broken.

- I am incomplete

Deep wounds

No matter how much pain you bring,
your hatred cannot keep me away.
I still fight,

-       to be in your veins.

Shamela Dad

Don't cry at my funeral.
I died the day you walked out of my life.
My funeral will be nothing.

-       Nothing but a formality.

Deep wounds

You said you would move heaven and earth for me.

-    Yet you dragged me through hell.

Shamela Dad

Love can be a murderous game.
Left in the darkness,

-     feeling insane.

Deep wounds

Those midnight thoughts never seem to escape my mind.
I'm always thinking, wondering why.
Why is my mind a ticking time bomb of pain?
I feel the sadness and emptiness exploding within me.
Feeling alone and cold.
It's like I'm the enemy of my own living.

- The creator of this darkness I now live in.

Deeply wounded.

\-   Unable to die.

Deep wounds

You taught me how to love.

-    teach me how to forget.

Shamela Dad

He is no longer my love.
He is a monster.

-     A devil in disguise.

Deep wounds

My eyes search for you everywhere.

-    You're nowhere to be found.

Shamela Dad

I am a prisoner of your thoughts.

-    How can I let you go?

Deep wounds

A moment without you,

-    is another step closer to hell.

Shamela Dad

When you walked out my life,
I did everything to save myself.
But in the end, I was destroyed.

-    Destroyed by your hatred.

Deep wounds

I feel the hurt and torture deep within.
The searing pain of hate.
The sadness lingers thoroughly inside my soul.
So much anger burns within.
Seeking to destroy you,

-       with bittersweet revenge.

Shamela Dad

I was art.

-   My artist had been another.

Deep wounds

You had always inflicted hurt upon her.

-   She embraced the beauty of the pain.

Shamela Dad

I could walk away from everyone I ever knew.

-    I can't walk away from you.

Deep wounds

She told him she loved him.
He stared at her in silence.
He slowly turned around and walked away.
That's the day her life ended.

-       She hoped she will find peace.

Shamela Dad

You always hear the saying,
'until death do us apart'
Maybe my death will bring us closer.
Maybe that's when you will realise what I meant to you.
Maybe that's when you will crave for me, just as I have
been longing for you.
It will be too late.
I will not return.
You will regret everything you put me through.
You wouldn't be able to make amends.
I will be at peace from the suffering I endured by loving
you.
But you,
you will die a death every day,

-    as you drown in your own guilt.

Deep wounds

His love was like fire.
A spark of raging passion.
But also, like fire, he burnt bridges.
He destroyed me.

-    An eruption of heartbreak.

Shamela Dad

Recovery

Deep wounds

My heart now holds
a tragic story. My heart
bleeds ink,

    - to write our poetry.

Shamela Dad

We should remember
that even though patience
is bitter,

    - the fruit will always remain sweet.

Deep wounds

Oh sweetheart;
You have one life.
Do you really want to
spend it chasing those
who don't even bother to
check up on you? Do you
really want to spend it
questioning and doubting
your love? The entire world is
in your hands. Let go of what's
destroying you. Oh sweetheart;
You have one life.

- Make it count.

Shamela Dad

I made you my world.
The day you left,
my world collapsed in to pieces.
Within time I realised that it
was best to let go and accept
that it wasn't meant to be.
Now I'm creating a brand-new world.
Even if it feels as if it's the end,

-     remember within time you will heal.

Deep wounds

Sometimes I want to keep feeling
the pain. It reminds me that I'm still
alive. It helps me to find that strength
from deep inside,

    - to survive.

Shamela Dad

I remember drowning in the deep
sea full of failure, fear and expectations.
But I knew this feeling will not last.
God reminded me that I can swim.

-    I can finally save myself.

Deep wounds

Patience is a virtue.
Not many of us see that.
It is when we decide to put
the pain on hold for a while, we
see things for how they truly are.
When we are waiting, we allow
the pain to lead us to where we need
to be.
Only with time can you heal and
grow.

- Be patient for it is a virtue worth owning.

Shamela Dad

When I need help,
I write to myself.
It is those words that
save me.

-   They help me heal.

Deep wounds

The deepest wounds leave
scars that never go. It just
shows that all the pain
and the endless suffering
is real. The scars become a
part of us as we accept things for how they are.

-      so that we can heal.

Shamela Dad

I've realised that healing takes
a long time.
I'm finally beginning to heal.
The pain is getting less and less.
The scars are fading.
My shattered heart is healing.
Now I live on hope
that one-day,

-    I'll be happy again.

Deep wounds

Today I breathe without you.
But instead of pain,
I feel serenity and calmness.

-    I am at the process of healing.

Shamela Dad

You will only begin
healing once you take
ownership,

-     of your problems.

Deep wounds

If you were ever so happy
with the wrong person,
imagine, just imagine
 the endless of happiness,

-       you'll feel with the right one.

I destroyed my demons,
I finally let go of all the
negativity.
I embraced the positivity.

- I learnt to smile.

Deep wounds

I felt a rush of sensation,
a sensation known as
happiness.
Something I have not felt,

-    in a very long time.

Shamela Dad

Pain is what inspired me,

-     to search for happiness.

Deep wounds

Someday we will find it.
It could take days, weeks,
months, or even years.
But we will find it.
Both our minds and hearts will
 be content.

-    Someday we will find happiness.

Shamela Dad

One door closes, and another will open.
I pray you walk
through the door that
leads you to happiness.

- You deserve it more than anything.

Deep wounds

Peace,

-   Will make our lives complete.

Shamela Dad

Keep your head up.
Don't let them bring you down.

-    It is you who is wearing the crown.

Deep wounds

No matter what you go through in life,

-       try to stay positive.

Shamela Dad

It was when I needed you
the most that you abandoned
me. I was lost.
I then found myself within writing.

-    That's when I felt peace.

Deep wounds

You look at me and all you
see is scars.
For me-
those scars tell a story about a battle.
My battle of survival in this cruel, insensitive and shallow
world.

- a battle I fought against myself

Shamela Dad

Now that you have walked away,
 I can't tell you how I feel.
All I can only do is write of you.
I know we may not be together
anymore.
But you will live here with me,

-   for as long as my hands can hold a pen.

Deep wounds

Think of your angel,
forget about the rest.
We all commit sins which
we regret. Time will come,
and you will feel again.
There's a heart deep inside
wanting to beat again.
Are you feeling cold? An empty soul.
Forget your pain, forget your
anguish.
Conquer your dreams and grab on to hope.

- A broken life can be rebuilt.

Shamela Dad

One day you will learn to
quit fighting fate.
You will learn to take
care of yourself.

-    You will learn to let go.

Deep wounds

You don't really forget about
your past,

-     you learn from it.

Shamela Dad

Whatever your struggle,
Whatever your pain,

-    remember there's sunshine after the rain.

Deep wounds

I wish it were possible
that you never experience
pain and sorrow, but you must.
If you let them, all your
sorrows will shape you in a
positive way.
You will trip, and you will fall.
The negativity will discourage you.
You will stand up, dust yourself off,
and take another step.

-    You are strong.

Shamela Dad

All I want back is what I have lost.
I want to be whole again.
I live on the hope that tomorrow
I'll find someone new,

-    to help place the missing pieces.

Deep wounds

A strong girl is reborn,

- ready to face the world.

Shamela Dad

Sometimes you must let go.
On your way down,
you will spread your wings.

-   You will learn to fly.

A mistake will remain a mistake
unless you learn from it.

-       Life lessons.

Shamela Dad

You were poison,

-    finally, I found my cure.

Deep wounds

My nightmares turned in to dreams,

-     when I let go of you.

Shamela Dad

I find solace in the words I write.
They are my saviour.
My home.

- Every letter becomes an escape.

Deep wounds

I will continue to live in patience.
In the end, the wait will be worth it.

-    Patience is my only weapon.

Shamela Dad

I will fix the cracks you left
between my ribcage
from when you pulled out my
wings.
Even though they are broken and tattered,
I will learn to mend them.

-    I will learn to fly again.

Learning

Shamela Dad

Time.
It is a healer,

-    for others it is a killer.

Deep wounds

Your thoughts,

-    I wear like my favourite outfit.

Knowing tough love lead her to hate herself.
She'd cry herself to sleep at night.
Her heart would bleed.
She would be forever longing to be freed.
She thinks of death as she feels so much pain.
She's starting to lose herself as she turns insane.
She lets out silent screams,
as she battles with her wildest dreams.
She told him how she has not got much to give, but she
wants him to be the reason she lives.
She tells him how he would not understand.
As tears rolled down her cheeks, he whispered,

-     come hold my hand.

Deep wounds

You must love yourself first,

-     before loving me.

Shamela Dad

How do we keep on going?
When even the possible,

- seems like the impossible?

Deep wounds

We all have our angel
who helps us
see the light at the end of the tunnel.
No matter how hard a situation may be.
We all need positive vibes around us.

- We need peace.

Shamela Dad

How do I rewrite the story I told myself every night?

-    to accommodate a plot twist I never expected.

Deep wounds

We are all intertwined in our desires.
Everyone is in it for themselves.
Everyone will surround you during the good times.
During the difficult times,

-      everyone will leave.

Shamela Dad

Why is it so hard to support one another?
Why is it so hard to give someone nothing more than a
smile?
Everyone is fighting a battle.
If you ever meet someone who is genuinely happy,
don't be resentful towards them.
You will never know what hell they were dragged through,

-       before reaching their heaven in life.

Deep wounds

Sometimes we will experience the
same pain repeatedly.
Not because life is cruel;
It is so that we can learn to face
our problems.
Otherwise they will haunt us,

- there will be no escape.

Shamela Dad

We always think that drowning is bad.
But is it really, if I want to drown
deep inside of your love?
What if I want to swim and be pulled in the deepest and
darkest part of your soul?
Would it be bad if I want the tides to wash me away to a
place outside the real world?

- A place where it can be just you and me.

Deep wounds

It took me a while to learn something new.
There isn't anyone who can fix my broken soul. Only I can
do it. All these years I drowned in pain, if only then I
knew.
Maybe then I wouldn't have suffered,

-     for so long.

Shamela Dad

The hurt you gave me cut me
deeply like a knife. My wounds
will heal,

- I will get on with life.

Deep wounds

My only wish is to want back what
I have lost.
In the process of trying to save you,
I lost myself.
I want to feel whole again.
I know the pain I feel is just substantial enough to get up
again.
It gives me hope that
one day I will find someone who
will reconnect my fallen pieces.

- Someone who will teach me to love again.

Shamela Dad

I have lost you.
But do you know what they say about the things which are
lost?
Within time they are found again.
I will find you again.
Maybe not in this life,

-     but I will be yours again.

Deep wounds

It is ironic –
Your love gave me the patience to hold on.
Your hatred gave me the strength to let go.

-    to move on.

We always force things in life.
Sometimes you must wait for beautiful things to come to you.
What is meant to be will be.

-    Whenever. Wherever. However.

Deep wounds

We all get hurt.
It's not the end of the world.
We need to take it for what it is.
We need to move on.
Those who hurt you, didn't deserve you.
One day, we will look back and wonder why we even
cared.
Those who left, did us a favour.
So, no it's not about getting hurt.
It's about what we learn after the process of getting hurt.

- We learn that life goes on.

Shamela Dad

The saddest and painful thing is having your heart broken.
It feels as if all the energy has left you.
It feels as if everything in life has lost all meaning.
You gave your heart and soul to this one person, and now
they are not there anymore.
So, tell me, how can my heart be whole again?
How do I get rid of this pain?
Will I ever be happy again?
How will I cope all alone?
All these questions run around your mind.
You need to realise, heartbreak of any kind will lead you
closer to God.
You will realise that even though you may feel ultimately
alone in the world,

- God is always there to comfort you.

Deep wounds

When will I learn to understand
that once a book is closed,
no matter how long after I reopen it,

-    the story will remain the same?

Shamela Dad

When the one you love has left you,
you can feel a part of yourself missing.
It feels as if a limb has been removed.
You do all you can to get rid of this empty feeling.
You want to function as normal, yet every day is a
torturous battle.
No matter how badly you want to get rid of the hollow
and empty feeling, you know the hole will be filled again
one day.
The pain will end.
You will heal.
The empty felling helps you to understand,

-    slowly you will be whole again.

Deep wounds

How strange is life?
Every day I would raise my hands to pray that I have you
in my life.
However,
I may have lost you,

- but I found God.

Shamela Dad

I fell apart piece by piece.
Nobody could see how the pain had consumed me.
I was going insane.
I felt lost.
I felt alone.
I reached out to God.
I realised if there's a will, there's a way.
I didn't allow the pain to eat me away.
I let it make me stronger.
I won't give up,
I will see this through.
The way you forgot about me,

-    I'll forget about you too.

Deep wounds

I know things may seem difficult and gloomy.
You may feel that life is turning its back on you.
Feeling tired as you suffocate in the darkness.
It feels as if all your happiness has disappeared.
You wonder how life can be cruel to a beautiful soul like
you.
Let go of all that sadness.
Attempt to fix your life.
Strengthen your heart.

- You will heal.

Shamela Dad

No more fighting against the truth.
No more denial.
I thought of you as my strength.
An anchor wrapped around my feet.
I refused to sink.
But now it's time for me to let loose of the ropes which
bound me to you.
I must set sail now.
I've got to move on and learn from my past.
It's time to accept what makes me who I am, so that I can
love myself.

-    So, I can learn to love again.

Deep wounds

Someone will come along when you least
expect it.
Maybe, just maybe they will heal those wounds inflicted on
your broken heart.
Slowly those wounds will become scars.
A constant reminder that once broken,

-    you can be fixed again.

Shamela Dad

Every time I swam to the surface,
my emotions dragged me back down.
I was drowning in endless sadness.
But then you came along.
I saw the light.
I grabbed on to you for dear life as I made it back to land,

- a land of happiness.

Deep wounds

They say patience is key.
Then why are we always sick of waiting?

-      we are patients of patience.

Shamela Dad

Sitting next to you today after so long,
was everything.
There were no words necessary.
The silent spoke in volumes.
This poem is for you.
Let me get this off my chest.
You deserve happiness,

-   you deserve to shine.

Deep wounds

One day you will be happy.
You will feel at peace.
You will find love.
The type of love which will grow like a flower.
It will bloom in the sunlight,

    -    it will keep growing even in the rain.

Shamela Dad

Sometimes I want your chest to feel tight.
I want you to feel suffocated.
Feel pain at the sound of my name.
That is how I feel every time your name is mentioned.
You tossed me aside like I didn't mean anything to you.
Sometimes I wish you know how I feel.
But it will destroy me to ever see you hurt.

-     I pray you remain pain free.

Never give up on your goals.
Never give up on your dreams.
Put your mind to it,
and you will achieve.

- Sometimes dreams are the only thing that a
  person has.

Shamela Dad

Do not compare yourself with other people.

-    we all have our time to shine.

Deep wounds

She was left in darkness.
But she finally found the light.
Like a wilting rose,
she slowly started to regain her strength after years without
the sun.
She was healing,

- She began to blossom.

Shamela Dad

Anyone can make me laugh,

-    but you gave me true happiness.

What is love?
The question on everyone's lips.
To love is to have that one special soul.
The one who you can always depend on.
To be there by your side throughout the years.
Sharing the laughter as well as the tears.
My partner, my lover but most importantly my best friend.
You taught me the full meaning of loving and caring.
Proved that all dreams do come true.
I learnt my meaning of love,

-     the day I met you.

You always say I deserve better.
Maybe you're right,
maybe I do.
But it won't be the same if it isn't you.
Let me tell you how that isn't true.
It doesn't even matter who the 'better' person is. You
see, I need someone who makes a better me.

-    You make me a better person.

And now it is time to put yourself first.
Let go off all the bad times.
Switch off the negativity.
Focus on your goals.
Reach for the moon.
Do whatever pleases you,

- you are the master of your own destiny.

Shamela Dad

You will find the courage to walk away.
You will find the courage to forget.
You will find the courage to do right.

-    the courage to begin again.

You will fall apart.
All that matters is that you hold yourself together
again.
You will crumble down and fall,
Make sure you stand up tall.

-      The meaning of survival.

Shamela Dad

You lose loved ones.
Those who said that they would always be there.
It hurts.
It rips you apart internally.
You feel as if you don't know how to cope.
But darling,
You fail to realise,
maybe they left because you were toxic for them.
Or maybe they were toxic for you.
We see the bad,
yet we never see the good.
We can't change what's written,
and I can't stress that enough.
Sometimes it's healthy to cut ties.
Sometimes we lose others,

-    so that we can find ourselves.

Deep wounds

I used to be afraid to sleep as I knew my nightmares will
be there waiting for me.
It took me a while to realise,
there's no difference between my nightmares and dreams.
They both give me hope,

-      they teach me how to live.

Shamela Dad

This one's for you.
The one who helped me see right from wrong.
The one who stood by my side all along.
You found me lost in the darkness,
you helped me see the light.
Life had made me weak to my knees,
You taught me to use that to my advantage.
You told me to pray the pain away.
It's ironic,
You came in to my life as a lesson and a blessing.
A lesson that there are beautiful souls in the world.
A blessing as you showed me the right path.
I pray for your happiness.
I pray for your success.
I will never forget all that I learnt from you.
This one's for you, my best friend.

-   Nemo

Destroy the label

Depression is one of the most prevalent mental health disorders across the world. Did you know that it is estimated that about 10 to 15 percent of children and teens are depressed at any given time? How many of these children seek help? How many have the strength to open their hearts out to their parents? That's the problem, even in this generation everyone is afraid to speak out, they are worried about being the odd one out. Why, why is mental health seen as a taboo? Stigma this, stigma that, it is time to destroy that label. Many fail to realise that stigma and discrimination can worsen someone's mental health problems. The fear of speaking out can delay them from getting help and possibly receiving treatment. Many people believe that people with mental ill health are violent and dangerous. Did you know that they are more at risk of being attacked? They are most likely to harm themselves rather than harming other people.

For all you beautiful souls out there suffering, I urge you please seek help. Don't, I repeat DON'T let stigma create self-doubt and shame. Reach out to people you trust for the compassion, support and for understanding your needs. It is time to speak out against stigma. The purpose of this chapter is to express feelings based around stigma and to raise awareness. I really hope this can give you the courage to speak up and not suffer in silence. I want to show you that you are NOT alone, others all over the world are facing similar challenges. Alongside the help of 9 amazing writers, I want to show the world that seeking support and helping educate others can make a big difference.

Like an uninvited guest, depression came knocking. You feel like a helpless and hopeless victim while society is a dictator. Telling you how you should feel and what you should not feel. Feeding you poison, telling you it's not real. You don't know what to do with the feelings inside, you put on a mask and learn to hide. Ever so hypocritical right? The world tells us to face our fears, yet they make us hide our fears. They're scared of what everyone will say. It's so much easier to smoke yourself to death, not to eat and learn to cut. You know why? It's so difficult to open your mouth and speak. Reality feels so out of reach. Shouldn't be afraid of those who look at you wrong, let their negativity make you strong. When is the world going to realise that stigma is a taboo? It can be your reality too. Ill mental health is not a disease;
MENTAL HEALTH MATTERS AND SO DO YOU!

-@deepwoundsx

Shamela Dad

Depression isn't all about sadness and crying, more about
smiling whilst dying.
It's like you try so hard yet still don't succeed, help you
don't want but perhaps you need.
You don't want to grab onto a hand, for you'll become a
burden, but being alone
this'll only worsen. Blinded by darkness you still try to
fight, there's no harm in asking
for a helping hand, to bring you back to the light.

  - @saif.writes

Deep wounds

I used to curl up in a ball in the middle of my bed holding
my head down trying to escape the darkness only to find
myself amidst more darkness. Was there no end to the
pain? To the sadness? Was there no happy ending for my
soul? I was drowning in my own mind and every time I
tried to resurface I sunk further. Did I ever hit the ground?
Or did I keep drowning until there is nothing of me left?
Neither. I kept fighting and fighting. I found anchors in
my friends to haul me up out of the black Sea and break
the surface, where I once again felt the sunlight dance on
my skin. There was a happy ending for this lost soul. And
there will be a happy ending for every one of you. I know
it is easy said than done but, darling, just hold tight and
swim a little harder each day. Because one day you'll break
the surface and find yourself in calmer waters, smiling.

   - @rollsroses

We're all in our own battles that rattle the deepest corners
of our minds, the people around us blind.
Every one of us has our own struggles and hardships, so
be kind.
We live in an illusion of a world, so just like the past
eventually became the past, nothing ever really lasts.

   - @hk.writes

Darling let me tell you a little secret; reach your hand out
and give people a shout.
You're not alone so there's no need to suffer in silence.
Instead it's your life that you need to balance. Don't be
afraid to speak because you are not weak. You're
amazing please don't forget that. I know life is hard and
things will get tough but everything will be okay, one day.
But we have to take every day as it comes. Smile,
laugh and be with those who make you happy. Your soul is
beautiful and kind.
Cherish every day. We'll be here today but will we be here
tomorrow? As the sun rises, the day is full of surprises.
So, smile dear one as the day is beautiful and great things
are to come.

-@S.O

Depression will eat you, so close your eyes and let your heart speak. Break your mind with peace and laugh with happiness. Seek help as these therapists will only bring you back to Home. Your loved ones are part of you, so my love reach out to them and believe your mind is just a little game. Some days it's bad, and other days it's good. Mental health illnesses are just like dark days, they'll eat you, but the light will always take you into the clouds. Bring the light back into you, my love.

-@xsywritesx

Deep wounds

I wish I could explain what happens in my brain when I
think about things that don't carry a bulb or a switch to
turn the light on. It's as if I'm surrounded by darkness that
neither you nor I could overcome. Living in my brain is a
constant chaos, destruction and you never know when
you're going to fall into a deep old trap.
But you'll see this light someday.
Don't forget to grab hold of it and that will lead the way
out, remember nothings temporary and neither is our
depression.
You will smile truly one day, I promise.

-@unpublishedwords

We suffer in silence, at the hands of this internal violence.
Voices inside of our head, saying things we never said.
Echoing sadness so masked outside, not a single soul
to ask if you're alright. Just more whispers about why you
haven't been speaking, they don't understand the nights
are spent weeping. That you're slowly breaking, that this is
so much more than faking, please listen to me,
this is real aching.

-@TheSmilingAkh

Deep wounds

Surrendering to the pain that the world offers is not a sign of weakness, it is a sign of tiredness; however, it's also a sign of disparity and realisation that no one else will come to your rescue apart from yourself. So, endure the pain and have faith in yourself, be the catalyst for a better tomorrow, as there the battle you are facing will soon end. They'll come to a halt and everything bitter will become beautiful and sweet.

-@akhthatwrites_

Shamela Dad

Dear depression.

you ended my life many times
I have seen parts of me die
before my actual death
you have always ended me
but given me reasons to wake up
and begin my life again
to begin breathing again
to begin healing again
all in the next morning
I will never kill myself
but I will always kill the old me.

- @saidnotspoken

ABOUT THE AUTHOR

While reading this you will get to know me.
Every letter you read will unite together with my soul.
Within every line you read, my pain resides.
Every word represents a light.
Yes, dark days will occur so will the pain.
This is a message for those who understand,
we can be strong, and we will carry on.

Follow on Instagram - @deepwoundsx

27256745R00094

Printed in Poland
by Amazon Fulfillment
Poland Sp. z o.o., Wrocław